HUNTER AND NOAH VS. SASQUATCH

SASQUATCH CHRONICLES
BOOK 3

PATRICK TALMADGE

HANGAR 1 PUBLISHING

1

TRUSTING THE LITTLE REDHEAD WESTERN GIRL

Grandpa jumped into the irrigation canal with Hunter, Noah, their mom, and their dad. That was when Mom heard the little redhead western girl yelling, "They want you!" Mom decided she'd had enough and would be taking the boys back home, right then and there. Dad and Grandpa wisely chose to follow. The first thing Grandpa heard when he resurfaced was the little redhead western girl, who had been with the Sasquatch, yell, "I made a mistake, they don't just want you... they want to teach you!"

By the time Grandpa realized what the girl had said, the family had drifted down the irrigation canal and around a bend, so he could not see or hear the girl any longer. Grandpa was floating along in the swift current, trying to decide what to do.

It was Mom who spoke first, "Did anyone else hear the girl say they wanted to teach us or the kids besides me?"

Everyone agreed that she'd said that.

"But what does 'teach you' mean? It's my summer vacation from school and I am not ready to go back to class yet," whined Noah.

"I, for one, would like to climb out of this canal, go back to the tree, and see if we can make contact from the safety of being up there," said Grandpa. "Assuming the Sasquatches' time speed difference doesn't mess it up," he added.

Mom looked at Grandpa long and hard before she said, "if you and Dad can promise to keep these boys safe, I will agree to go back now. I am concerned about the little girl... but one hint of danger and I am dragging my boys home immediately."

"I promise to do everything in my power to prevent anything from happening to the boys. Looks like we will need to use our safety lines to snag a tree branch," Grandpa said calmly, as he pulled his safety line out.

"I have you all beat," said Noah, as he pulled out his fishing slingshot. "I might not be great at catching fish, but I can shoot that branch with my arrow. I just hope my fishing line is strong enough to hold my weight!"

The whole family watched as Noah's arrow struck the branch. Once the slack came out of his line, he was body surfing. Turns out there was more water than a couple weeks ago, so the current was running faster, leaving Noah skimming and spinning out of control on top of the water. Luckily, Noah's fishing line wasn't strong enough to hold him. It broke after giving him a good ride for a few seconds.

When Noah broke loose, he was laughing hard, as was his family who couldn't believe he had just done that, but were happily laughing at his antics and relieved to see that he wasn't hurt.

"Nice try, Noah," said Grandpa. "You were correct to wonder whether the fishing line would hold your weight. For future reference, you weigh 70 pounds, and the fishing line is rated for 20. As your impromptu test showed, no, your fishing line will not stop or hold you. Your safety line, on the other hand, is designed to do exactly as the name implies," Grandpa said sarcastically.

Noah had caught up to everyone by the time Grandpa finished teasing him, and said, "If I can make a request, Grandpa, would you please install 80-pound fishing line on my fishing slingshot?" I think I may have found a fun use for it!"

"Sure, Noah, I'll get right on it after we escape the Sasquatch, and that will be sometime after we can get out of this darn canal and dry off," Grandpa said, as he tickled Noah.

After they'd climbed out of the irrigation canal and dried off, it was time to have a family meeting. Noah complained about how the weak fishing line had ruined his idea, and Hunter quipped back that it might have more to do with his weak mind. That's what started the pinecone fight that the whole family joined in on.

When they were done throwing pinecones, everyone collapsed next to the canal in a fit of laughter. Noah was the first to break the silence, by asking when they were going to eat. Hunter reminded Noah that if he hadn't broken his fishing line, he could have shot fish.

"Instead of wasting time talking here, let's walk back to our tree, eat, and plan how we are going to approach Tina and the

Sasquatch. Oh, and I suggest you two boys get your other fishing gear ready to catch us some fresh fish," Mom said.

Dad helped get Hunter and Noah heading towards the tree, as Mom and Grandpa led the way. It took almost an hour to get back to the tree. Once they arrived, Mom divided up the chores. She sent the boys out to catch fish, Dad to the river to get crayfish and clams, and Grandpa to collect berries, nuts, and mushrooms, while she set up the kitchen and preheated the solar oven. Once all the food had been gathered, she set about cooking with Hunter and Noah's help, while Grandpa and Dad began planning their next moves.

"We need to figure out how and where the Sasquatch time speed changes, and the relationship it has with the valley and our tree, if we are going to be able to talk to the girl. From experience I can tell you that, if we aren't close enough, they won't be able to hear us in real time and so we may need to go all the way down to the valley floor," Grandpa proposed, while scratching his chin.

Dad sighed before responding. "Getting Mom to allow her boys anywhere near those 8-foot-tall hairy beasts, even with the little girl, will be a challenge... I'm just hoping we can find a way to communicate from the safety of our tree."

"After they picked up my crawler like it was an empty bag, I am also a bit apprehensive about being within their reach," said Grandpa. "The fact that 100 of your company's employees, including guards with weapons, disappeared without a trace makes me even more cautious.

"What if you and I sat down in the valley waiting for them, while Mom, Hunter, and Noah stayed in the tree?"

"I thought about that also, but until we know how the distance from the valley floor to the tree affects time, we can't take that chance. If the people down in the valley are down too long, then time would pass at a faster rate for them than the people in the tree. We need to do a few experiments to determine our best course of action. It may turn out that we all will have to go down there if we hope to stay in the same time speed."

"I think we need to practice with our electric safety ropes," said Noah, cutting in. "We need lots of practice so that, if something happens, we can escape really fast."

"Maybe, if we got attacked by the Sasquatch, we could throw Noah at them and escape," Hunter said. "Heck, they want him badly, so they would stop to grab him, then we could zoom up the tree and be safe!" Hunter then immediately had to duck a fast-flying pinecone.

"The next pinecone thrower will not be eating lunch, dinner, or breakfast for the remainder of our stay in this tree! If that is understood, you should all wash up for lunch," Mom barked.

"Is there a time limit on that pinecone throwing restriction?" asked Noah.

Mom shot a sideways glance at Noah that Hunter thought would have scared even the Sasquatch. Noah looked at Mom, realized she was being serious, and said, "Well, I guess that answers my question. There is no way I am going to eat my own cooking when mom's here," though he said the second part under his breath as he washed.

"That boy lets his stomach do the talking, just like your dad did when he was his age," Grandpa said to Hunter as they washed up.

"I am pretty sure I've never seen you miss a meal either, Grandpa," said Hunter.

"That may be true, because I have learned never to go hungry when you don't have to."

"Let's have less talking and more washing before your lunch gets cold, and I have to throw it to the Sasquatches," said Mom.

In his hurry to be first to fill his plate, Noah tripped. It was not an ordinary trip, but a top-of-the-line funny trip. Noah's safety line was hanging a bit too low, because he hadn't rolled it in all the way in last time he was practicing, and the hook caught a branch, which caused the line to go taunt, and trip him. That would have been funny enough, but when he stood up and hit the line release, it released so quickly he stumbled backwards. The tree top nest's bottom being curved like a bowl increased his speed as he fell forward, and then continued stumbling until he toppled over the edge. The last thing Noah heard was Mom's scream.

Grandpa was sure that, if the Sasquatch were within 100 miles, they would have heard that scream. At least that might get them here, he thought, as he rushed to the edge to check on Noah. Before he was halfway across the nest, Grandpa heard laughing. They were not giggles, but deep hysterical laughter. Not only was Noah not hurt, but he was laughing hard, from somewhere over the edge of the nest.

As luck would have it, the locking clip on Noah's safety line had gotten caught on a branch and stopped him from falling too far. After he realized he wasn't going to hit the ground,

Noah had started laughing. Mom wasn't quite as happy, and the way she told Dad and Grandpa to haul him back up caused Noah to hit reverse on his electric winch and drop to the ground by the irrigation canal.

"You can run, but you can't hide," Mom called out, as she once more walked to the edge of the nest, hooked her safety line to a thick branch, looked at Dad, Grandpa, and Hunter, and said solemnly, "Don't ask questions if I come back alone," then turned and jumped. "I'm coming for you, runt!"

"If I didn't know better, I'd say Mom loves jumping with that safety line setup," said Dad.

"Maybe, but I'm glad it's Noah and not me she's chasing," said Hunter.

2

FINDING THE LIMITS OF THE SASQUATCH TIME EFFECTS

After Mom and Noah returned, everyone ate lunch and began planning how to test the boundaries of the Sasquatch time effects. It was decided Hunter and Grandpa would go down to the valley floor, at the base of the tree, and remain there for one hour. Grandpa would have to guess the time, because they didn't have any electronics that worked. For the first test, they would stay within 20 feet of the cliff wall. Grandpa and Hunter would carry on a constant conversation and see if Mom, Dad, and Noah could hear it. Likewise, Mom, Dad, and Noah would try talking and see if Hunter and Grandpa could hear them. Once lunch was finished, and the dishes cleaned, Hunter and Grandpa descended the tree to begin the first boundary time check.

Hunter and Grandpa talked in the valley, then climbed back up after what they guessed was an hour. When they asked Mom, Noah, and Dad if they had heard their conversation, the reply was negative. To them it'd seemed like the pair had only just left.

"What do you mean, we just left?" We've been gone for at least an hour down in the Sasquatch valley," Grandpa said, looking shocked.

"I swear you two left no more than 20 seconds ago," said Mom.

"Really, Grandpa, I didn't even have time to get to the edge of the nest to watch you two go down there before you came back up," said Noah.

"So... how come when Tina, the little redhead western girl, and the Sasquatch walk by or stop and eat, we can hear them, but you couldn't hear or see us?" Grandpa wondered aloud.

"Either the Sasquatch change the time speed difference when they are walking through here, or we need to move further away from the wall. It is possible that the time energy builds up, kinda like a strong river current alongside a steep cliff wall, exactly like water would against a steep riverbank," Grandpa theorized then paused for a second and sighed before continuing. "Well, Hunter, looks like we need to go back out and try talking again, but this time further away from the cliff wall, like somewhere near the middle of the valley."

"Sounds fine to me, and hey, maybe we can bring a snack to munch on," Hunter grinned.

"Sure, I get accused of only thinking about food all the time, but when anyone else does it's fine," said Noah.

One look from Mom and Noah clammed up, while Hunter grabbed a few snacks for himself and grandpa.

"I expect the two of you to keep your eyes wide open for

Sasquatch while you're out there, and both of you better be ready to run back to the tree, Hunter," she said in a flat, serious tone.

"Mom, it's going to be fine," Hunter said, as he climbed down ahead of Grandpa.

By the time Noah made it to the edge of the nest, he saw Grandpa and Hunter already sitting out in the middle of the valley, talking and eating their snacks.

"I'm not sure how they got there so fast, but Grandpa and Hunter are already out there sitting down and eating," said Noah.

"What are you talking about, Noah? You better not be fooling around here," said Mom, as she hurried to the nest edge to get a look for herself.

Mom gasped when she saw Noah was telling the truth.

Dad reached the edge of the nest right after her, and when he looked over the edge, all he could say was, "How could they possibly have gotten there so fast?"

Noah said, "I can hear them talking, but not well enough to make out what they are saying."

"Try yelling to them, Noah," said Dad.

Noah tried yelling half a dozen times to get their attention. Mom and Dad then both tried yelling a few times, but it was apparent that neither Grandpa nor Hunter could hear them, so they sat silently in the tree and watched. After a few minutes, Hunter and Grandpa stood up and headed back towards the tree. Dad guessed that no more than 2 seconds had passed from the time Grandpa and Hunter disappeared beneath the tree to when they reached the tree top nest. It was so quick that, when

Hunter climbed into the nest followed by Grandpa, it scared Mom.

"After testing and considering our options, I believe we need to go down into the valley as a whole family to make this work. First, the Sasquatch do not appear to be interested in Dad and I. Second, we do not want to get separated and wind up in different time speed places. If all five of us go down, we can stay in the same time speed, and then we will be most likely to attract the Sasquatch and Tina, and Mom will feel that Hunter and Noah are safer," Grandpa said, sounding surer of himself than he had in a while.

"I am not too keen on Hunter and Noah going anywhere near the Sasquatch, but I believe we need to make sure Tina is safe. With Grandpa and Dad's help, we should be safe, so I agree that going down into the valley as a family is the move here," said Mom.

"I don't know about Dad and Grandpa protecting Hunter and I, but I sure can attest to the Sasquatch being afraid of you, Mom," said Hunter. "Oh, my goodness, Dad, you should have seen the Sasquatch back away from Mom when they got between her, Noah, and I. She was shaking her garden spade at them like it was a sword, yelling and threatening them. They looked genuinely scared of her."

"We don't know how long it will take for the Sasquatch to find us, so we might plan on staying down in the valley until they do," said Grandpa. "Our suits will be fine for warmth and protection at night, but we should each make a nice fern and grass padded bed.

Noah and Hunter were super excited about camping in the

valley after having been stuck sleeping in the tree for so many days. Mom was not happy about leaving her running water and shower, but her concern for Tina gave her the courage to give up her creature comforts. Dad and Grandpa gathered the items they thought they would need to camp in the valley. Lastly, Grandpa went over the safety features of the suits once more, just in case they needed to use any of them. Noah was still complaining about how he couldn't shoot an arrow into a branch and winch himself up out of trouble because his line wasn't strong enough. This irritated Hunter, who was tired of his brother's whining, so much that he suggested he try it anyway, because without the extra drag from the water it might work. Hunter could feel three sets of adult eyes burning a hole in his back, and decided to tell Noah his line was still too weak, and hopefully not get in trouble for his suggestion. Grandpa wanted to get an early start the next day, so instructed everyone to begin preparing that night tonight so they could depart on their trip to the valley right after breakfast.

Mom wasn't sure she'd slept at all that night, what with being so worried about the Sasquatch trying to steal Hunter and Noah the next day. Dad held Mom's hand all night. That helped, but she was still worried as she made breakfast. After breakfast, Grandpa had everyone gather their gear and run through their safety checks. Once all the safety checks were complete, the food was packed, and Mom had calmed down, the family left the safety of the tree nest. Noah led the way down the tree as usual, followed by Grandpa, Hunter, Mom, then Dad. Noah had tried arguing that everyone should leave the tree using their safety lines and electric winches, so they would have more practice, but Grandpa had then pointed out that Noah and Mom had gotten plenty of practice lately, and so maybe it would be best to practice climbing down instead.

As planned, after everyone had reached the Sasquatch valley floor, they regrouped at the base of the tree to determine their next move. Grandpa suggested they stay close to their tree on the first night, just in case anything unexpected happened. Once everyone was safely down, Mom saw a huge tree that had a small pond near the opposite side of the valley. She had everyone gather in the shade of that large tree to plan, by a small pond about 400 feet from their tree.

3

MEETING THE SASQUATCH AND THE WESTERN GIRL

Grandpa wanted them to always remember to stay close to one another. That was the only way they wouldn't have any more time differences. He also felt they needed to stay on the valley floor, so they would be in the same time speed as the Sasquatch. If they were to have a chance to meet Tina and the Sasquatch, so they could talk, then for sure staying on the valley floor was necessary.

The weather was warm, and there was no chance of rain for days, so everyone gathered grass and ferns to make soft beds under the tree for the night and didn't worry themselves with constructing a shelter. It was too early for lunch, so after everyone picked a spot and made their beds, it was time for a walk around the area. Grandpa felt that if they walked around the valley for a while, they'd have a better chance of alerting the Sasquatch. Part of him wasn't comfortable with the thought of meeting Sasquatch, but his curiosity about the western girl gave him the courage to face the giants.

They had been walking for 20 minutes when they came to a garden filled with fruit trees, berry bushes, a vegetable patch, and a small stream. In the middle of the garden was a long stone table, big enough to accommodate up to 6 humans... or possibly a similar number of Sasquatch-sized bodies. Grandpa thought that it was odd to have seating for 6 humans, since they had only seen the one western girl, or maybe they had more humans?

Mom suggested they collect some of the wonderful food growing around them for dinner. Grandpa agreed, but wanted to stay there to eat at the table. It was obvious this was a frequently used eating area by the looks of it. If they were lucky, the Sasquatch may show up to eat.

"I am not so sure about eating with any Sasquatch... from the looks of them, they will eat all the food," Noah said, with a serious look only a hungry young boy could have.

"See, Mom, all he ever thinks about is food," said Hunter.

"Yeah, and all you ever think about is your old lady girl-friend," Noah cut back.

It only took one look from Mom for both boys to clam up and begin collecting food for dinner. Dad and Grandpa looked at one another and grinned, both glad they weren't the focus of Mom's ire at that moment.

Everyone had been gathering food for an hour, and arranging it on the table, when Mom suddenly said, "We have visitors, everyone."

When he turned to look towards where Mom was looking, Grandpa saw five large Sasquatch, one small Sasquatch, and the western girl walking towards them. It appeared the group had come out of a cave in the cliff wall 20 feet away from where the table was. Grandpa was sure the cave wasn't there before. It was like the cliff had opened up and pushed him through and then closed on their first visit. The Sasquatch must have figured out how to dematerialize and re-materialize things like rock. "Well, if they can control time, why not rocks too?" Grandpa muttered.

Mom said, "I am not sure what Sasquatch eat, but I am grateful we picked so much food, because we have enough to share, if they eat fruits and vegetables. But, oh my, what if they eat meat... like people?" Mom asked, in a nervous voice.

"Hey, I think that is my big Sasquatch friend," said Noah, as he walked up to one of the huge Sasquatch and held up his hand to high five it.

To everyone's surprise, the Sasquatch high fived Noah back. Noah then held his arms up high, motioning for the Sasquatch to pick him up. The Sasquatch looked at Noah, then to the little redhead western girl, who nodded her head. The Sasquatch bent down and picked Noah up. The look on Noah's face said it all. He was ecstatic, and snuggled into the Sasquatch's hairy chest.

"This is like having the biggest teddy bear in the world, and it can walk," shouted Noah.

Grandpa noticed that the Sasquatch seemed to be enjoying having Noah cuddling it. It was smiling and hugging Noah like a parent would a small child. The other Sasquatch was standing silently by, watching the heartwarming scene unfold. The little western girl was smiling, too. Meanwhile, Mom, Dad, and Grandpa were staring at 10-year-old Noah in the arms of an 8-foot-tall Sasquatch, and Hunter was transfixed by the western girl.

Mom looked at the incredible sight in silence for a moment, before finding her words.

"Is anyone hungry? Would everyone would like to sit down and enjoy it?"

The western girl smiled and said, "I am hungry, thank you, and my friends would also surely enjoy some of the wonderful food you gathered."

Once everyone was seated at the large table, four more Sasquatch appeared out of the cave, each carrying large platters. The Sasquatch with the platters walked around the table, setting plates and bowls next to everyone seated. The bowls and plates held all sorts of berries, nuts, and what appeared to be some sort of bread. Once the four Sasquatch finished serving everyone, they disappeared back into the cave.

"Everyone, please feel free to enjoy the bounty placed before you and thank you all who helped to gather and prepare," said the little western girl.

Noah didn't need a second invitation, and began stuffing his face with all the new foods the Sasquatch brought. "Oh, wow! This bread is fantastic," Noah said, through a greedy mouthful of food.

"My oh my," said Mom. "Noah is right, this bread is absolutely delicious."

The Sasquatch and the little western girl watched with

smiles as the rest of the family enthusiastically dug into the food.

Mom looked at one of the Sasquatch and asked, "Is there any way I could get the recipe for this bread?"

The Sasquatch smiled, then looked at the western girl, who said, "These gentle beings do not talk much, but they understand what you say."

"I am very sorry, we forgot to introduce ourselves. This is my youngest son, Noah, and his older brother is named Hunter."

"And that is Grandpa, Dad, and Mom," said Noah, between mouthfuls of food.

Everyone began to laugh then, even the Sasquatch, who seemed to always be in a pleasant mood. When the little western girl stopped laughing, she said her name was Tina, and that her friends didn't have names, because their society did not use names.

Grandpa asked Tina if the Sasquatch were able to talk and she told him they could, but rarely did unless absolutely necessary, like when they were teaching.

"I imagine their language is complex, considering the level of technology they possess," said Grandpa.

"Believe me, their words can be very big and hard to understand when they are talking science. It has taken many years spent living with them for me to totally understand them."

"I hope you don't mind me asking, but how long have you been with the Sasquatch, and how did you end up with them?" asked Grandpa.

"What is 'Sasquatch'?" asked Tina.

"Sasquatch is one of the names we call your tall, hairy

friends. Although until just recently no one has seen a Sasquatch, well... that is, except you," said Grandpa.

"Oh! Sasquatch is a pretty name for them," said Tina. "Even though they don't have names for themselves, I think they might like you already having names for them. As for how long I have been with the Sasquatch, well, I can't be sure. It has certainly been a long time, because I was only five years old when they found me. For some reason, I remember the year as 1857. That might have been the year we left Ohio for Washington. I remember riding on the wagon train for many days, along the Oregon Trail. We had stopped to rest after a long climb up a steep four-mile-long hill. It had been two days since we passed a little town called Tenino in Washington, on our way to Seattle. I was thirsty and wanted a drink, so I took a walk to the small river that ran a ways away from the wagon. After drinking my fill, I wanted to wash my hands, so I stepped into the river, but it was deeper and faster than it looked. Next thing I knew, I was being washed downstream. The water was freezing cold. After a few minutes of trying to swim, I went under. I can't remember a thing after that, until I woke up surrounded by my friends here."

"Did you say you remember the year 1857 as the year you left Ohio?" asked grandpa.

"I think so... but it was a long, long time ago, and I was very young."

"That certainly was a long time ago," said Grandpa.

"What year is it now then? Time passes differently here, so it is hard to know how long it's been."

Noah blurted out, "It's 2023, so that means you are almost

200 years old! That is way too old for Hunter. Even Grandpa isn't that old, and he is the oldest person ever!"

"Noah, you hush up and mind your manners young man! Obviously, Tina is the same age as your brother, so please mind your words," Mom said sternly, staring at him in a way that made him know she would've shouted if they weren't around strangers.

Noah was about to say something when Dad piped in, "You might want to listen to your mom, Noah. I am pretty sure you pushed it a bit too far this time, and Mom has had enough."

Tina was staring off into space, clearly digesting what Noah had rudely said, when Grandpa asked, "Did your time with the Sasquatch seem like a long time, or did it pass quickly, and do you know why you didn't age normally?"

Grandpa's questions brought Tina back to reality, and she thought for a moment before answering.

"Honestly, the time flew by! I was always having fun, learning interesting things, and traveling, so it really didn't seem to be 10 years, let alone 170. They told me they didn't want me to get too old, in the event I was reunited with other humans. And, well, I have met a few humans over the years, but they were all too old for me to properly socialize with. The Sasquatch felt it would be better for me to be introduced to humans near my age, so when Hunter and Noah came into the valley, they got excited. Maybe a bit too excited, because they told me that they had separated Grandpa from Hunter and Noah and set up all the previous troubles. This time they sent me out to see if I could make you feel comfortable enough to come out of hiding."

"We would still be hiding, too, but Hunter loves you and wants to marry you," said Noah, with a smirk, before his mom could stop him.

Both Hunter and Tina blushed immediately. Dad stood up, walked over to Noah, picked him up, threw him over his shoulder, and carried him off to give him a serious talking to.

While Tina and Hunter were blushing, Grandpa noticed the Sasquatch were smiling and looking at one another. Grandpa assumed they approved of the mutual crush that was evidently blossoming between the two kids. It made sense that the Sasquatch would want Tina to grow up as normal, with kids her own age, thought Grandpa, but he wondered how they kept her from aging.

By the time Dad brought the now silent Noah back to the table, Tina and Hunter had stopped blushing and were talking. It was obvious Hunter thought Tina—with her pale blue eyes, fiery red hair, and perfect smattering of freckles—was cute. Apparently, Tina thought Hunter was quite alluring also, because she never took her eyes off him as they talked. While everyone else silently ate their food, Tina and Hunter were eagerly asking each other questions and getting to know one another.

Mom and Dad, along with Grandpa, were enjoying seeing the two kids so happy and oblivious to everything but themselves. Dad must have read the riot act to Noah, because he was eating and not commenting.

4

GOING WITH THE SASQUATCH

Hunter looked at his mom and dad and said, "Tina said the Sasquatch have taught her almost every subject while she has been with them, and she even knows all sorts of advanced math that only college kids learn. She said they sat her in a chair, then put a weird hat with wires on her head, and that it made funny buzzing sounds, and then she learned fast without having to read, or do homework."

"That is not fair, I want to learn that way, too," said Noah.

"The Sasquatch would be honored for you to join them in the teaching center, Noah. They asked me to talk to Hunter and Noah and see if they wanted to spend time here to learn with them," Tina said.

"I am not very comfortable with the thought of my sons going into caves with these big fury guys, no matter how nice they seem now. What would happen if they got mad or hungry and tried to eat them?"

"You don't have to worry about the Sasquatch eating your boys, because they don't eat meat. They only eat fruits, vegetables and nuts," Tina managed to croak out amidst their deep laughter.

The Sasquatch themselves started laughing at Mom's comment, while shaking their heads no and holding up fruits and vegetables.

"Well... Noah is a bit nuts sometimes, so there may be trouble once in a while," said Grandpa, with a grin, which caused even more laughter from the Sasquatch.

Mom looked a bit embarrassed, and the small Sasquatch came over and gave her a hug. The small Sasquatch was Noah's size, and she had a unique white streak in her hair above her right eye. This small Sasquatch was Tina's closest friend, and they always seemed to be together. Mom thanked the small Sasquatch and offered a quick apology to the others, who graciously smiled and bowed in acknowledgment.

Grandpa looked at Tina, whose laughter had mostly trailed off, and asked her, "Would the Sasquatch allow me to go with Noah, and you to go with Mom, Dad, and Hunter? I can look out for Noah, which would make his parents feel more comfortable and also then I can learn more about the Sasquatch."

Tina and the Sasquatch all were nodding yes in response to Grandpa's question, and Tina said, "The Sasquatch would be honored to have you and Noah visit their home."

While plans were made for Grandpa and Noah to visit the Sasquatch, Noah and the small Sasquatch were off playing by the pond. The pair seemed to get along easily, like most young beings. Grandpa could tell Noah liked this young Sasquatch girl, because he was normally a loner, and yet seemed to be transfixed by this young being he'd only just met. Grandpa could see the young Sasquatch never spoke, but she and Noah didn't seem to have any problem communicating. Young beings are pure innocence, thought Grandpa, as he watched them play by the water with a smile on his face.

Tina suggested Grandpa and Noah go to their tree nest to collect anything they may want to bring back. Mom was still not too happy, and wanted to know how long Noah and Grandpa would be gone.

"The Sasquatch said they will be back in no time, and you will hardly miss them. Though I am not sure how long that is going to be, I trust that it will not be very long," said Tina, attempting to reassure her.

Grandpa called Noah over, and they went to the tree, along with the small Sasquatch girl and Tina, to gather a few things. Tina said the Sasquatch would provide everything they needed, and so to only bring things that they felt that would make them more comfortable.

"How long do you think we will be staying?" Grandpa asked Tina.

"That will be a question you and Noah will have to ask yourselves. You will be able to make a better informed decision once you visit the Sasquatch. There is so much they have to offer that it would be foolish for me to guess what you will enjoy, or for how long."

"I imagine their science and technology will be interesting enough to keep me busy forever," said Grandpa. "I am also pretty certain Mom won't allow us to be gone too long."

"Remember, they can adjust time to fit any situation you require. You only need to state your time requirements, and Mom's maximum time limit for being away from Noah, to the Sasquatch and they'll make that the length of your stay," said Tina.

"Dear me! We could be with the Sasquatch for years, but only a few minutes or hours will have passed for Mom and the others here," Grandpa said, with a wicked grin while thinking deeply. "I could even be with the Sasquatch for 10 years, which would only be a couple weeks or months for Noah, and just a few minutes for you here at the tree."

"I have no idea what you are talking about, but I know I want to stay with the Sasquatch and learn lots of cool stuff," Noah said, as he finished gathering a few things he wanted to take.

By the time Hunter, Mom, and Dad reached the tree top nest, Grandpa and Noah were ready to go. After many long hugs and goodbyes, the small Sasquatch led the way down the tree, followed by Noah and Grandpa. Tina remained up in the tree, and only she had an idea what was going to happen, and how amazing it would be. A smile came to her lips as she thought how much fun and exciting the future was going to be for her and her new family.

Mom watched Noah, Grandpa, and the small Sasquatch crawl out of the nest and down the tree to the valley with a few tears in her eyes. Before Mom or anyone else could say a thing, Noah came back up into the nest. Grandpa was right behind him, as was a large Sasquatch with the same white streak in its hair as the smaller Sasquatch that had just left a few seconds ago.

"What did you forget?" asked Dad.

"Mom, Dad, Hunter, and Tina, we have been gone for over 5 years," said Noah.

"No way... you guys just left 5 seconds ago," Hunter said.

"It was only a few seconds for you, my brother, but for us it has been much longer," said Noah.

"Oh my! You must be telling the truth... either that, or you both suddenly became quick change artists, because when you left a few seconds ago, you were wearing your custom Carhartt coveralls, and now you're dressed completely differently. Noah, except for the clothes, you look exactly the same, but Grandpa looks 20 years younger," Dad said, looking astonished.

"I am doing better than just looking younger, because the Sasquatch fixed most of my physical issues, even my bad knees! The Sasquatch have the most incredible science and technology. I feel fantastic! And I have been exercising and studying as well, like I haven't been able to in years!"

"Let me tell you about the learning center... it was fantastic. They can teach you any subject in a matter of a few weeks or months. Oh, and Mom, I may look like a 10-year-old, but I have spent most of the last five years studying every subject I possibly could. To be honest, Mom, it might be a waste of time for me to go into 4th grade, since I now have the equivalent of five college degrees."

Tina walked up to the Sasquatch with the white streak and gave her a hug. "My dear friend, you have grown up while you were gone."

"She wanted to age normally, now that you have a human family to live with. She has been your close friend, and so during that time it was best for her to remain your size in order to be more comfortable for you, but now is her time to grow and move forward."

"What do you mean, 'a family to live with'?" asked Tina.

"Tina, if you, Mom, Dad, and the boys are willing, the Sasquatch want us to bring you home with us," said Grandpa, "She has no living relatives, and she now needs humans to grow and mature properly. The Sasquatch have done all they can for her, and would like us to take care of her from here on out. As for the legality of bringing a lost orphaned girl home, well, the Sasquatch have been thoughtful enough to provide us with all the legal paperwork and even hacked into human computer systems to add Tina's new birth date and birth certificate."

"Oh, my! Yes, I would love to have you come live with us Tina!" said Mom, beaming as she hugged Tina, "Our home could use another girl. I bet you're much cleaner than the boys are, too."

"Before I spent five years with the Sasquatch, I would have teased that since Tina had already lived with hairy animals, she wasn't going to be as neat as me. Now, I have to admit Sasquatch are the cleanest and neatest beings I have ever known. Mom, you will be happy to know that the Sasquatch neatness has rubbed off on me a little bit... but don't expect miracles, I mean, they are good, but not that good," Noah said, with a smirk.

Tina was standing there, speechlessly staring at nothing. She had dreamed of having a family again but hadn't dared believe it would ever happen. She looked at Noah, Grandpa,

Dad, Hunter, and Mom, and said, "I would be honored to come live with you all, even Noah."

"The Sasquatch request that if we choose to leave and live away from here, we return once a month to check in," said Noah. "I for one am looking forward to the visits, because their food is the best!"

"Wait, aren't we forgetting a few things?" asked Dad.

"Like what?" asked Grandpa.

"Well, most importantly, all my company's personnel the Sasquatch have run away with, and then there's the 10 very expensive new drones," said Dad.

"Yes, there is the matter of 100 of Dad's company personnel that those big furry Sasquatch have been spoiling and educating. And yes, those old tech drones the Sasquatch have so generously modified extensively. They can now fly further and faster, as well as being undetectable. They can even now fly into outer space, and will be brought back when the men are finished with their education and training," said Grandpa.

"What do you mean 'education and training'?" asked Dad.

"The company personnel have been learning how to live on Earth in an environmentally neutral way, so they don't pollute and can instead live in true harmony with nature," said Grandpa. "The Sasquatch science and technology is remarkable. The personnel will return, along with the drones, very soon. The Sasquatch will be returning them to the dry riverbed one hour after they were taken. For everyone outside the valley, only one hour will have passed. The Sasquatch did not want the personnel's families to worry, or have it upset the company business operations. The Sasquatch were so impressed with how we came into their valley and then lived off the land. They could see we'd been training to be environmentally friendly, so they felt we were the perfect humans to announce themselves to. They also wanted to introduce Tina to us, so that she may grow up with us."

Despite having been studying with the Sasquatch for 2 years, Noah was still a 10-year-old boy and so couldn't help himself from suddenly blurting out, "Mom! I want to stay here, and I want to have my DNA changed so that I can grow hair like the Sasquatch, and so I don't have to wear clothes. Grandpa wouldn't allow me to have it done while we were with the Sasquatch, because he said I needed my mom and dad's permission first, so I'm asking now to get my DNA changed."

The look on Mom's face made Hunter start laughing so hard tears filled his eyes and he had to sit down or he'd keel over. Dad's reaction was even more intense. He had just taken a swig of his drink and proceeded to spray it all over the nest, with some shooting out his nostrils and landing on Mom. Seeing this made Hunter laugh even harder, which in turn made Dad totally lose control and laugh harder than he thought possible. By this time, both Grandpa and Noah had joined in on the out-of-control laughter. Mom glanced at them, stood up straight, put her hands on her hips, and made a huffing sound.

Noah looked at his mom and, even though he had been away for five years, realized how mad she was getting, and declared, "I'm out of here," then reached into his pocket, pulled out a thin strap with a hook on the end, wrapped it around a thick branch, and jumped over the edge of the nest.

"Under the circumstances, I believe Noah may be onto

something. That something is escaping quickly, which may reduce bodily injury. Apparently, he did learn something studying with the Sasquatch," said Grandpa, who then pulled a thin strap with a hook out of his pocket, attached it to a branch, looked at Dad and Hunter, and said, "A coward lives to fight another day," before jumping after Noah.

Hunter and Dad were both still laughing so hard they could barely stand. It took a few moments for them to figure out their safety rope releases, attach them, and jump. Before Dad jumped, he said, "Love you, honey, we're off to gather food for dinner, be back soon!"

Mom watched the four chickens bail out of the nest and chuckled to herself. It was good to keep them at least a little afraid of her. A little fear made them follow her orders more easily, she thought, with a little smile.

"Well, might as well get things ready to cook, since they are planning on gathering lots of special food to pacify me. Ah, how I love the power of being a strong woman," Mom said to herself, feeling content.

Dad got back first, with his mushrooms and berries, followed by Grandpa and Hunter. The pair had been to the river and brought back freshwater clams and crawdads. Just as Mom was about to ask where Noah had gotten to, a fur covered thing climbed into the nest and Mom screamed.

"It's just me, Mom, Noah, your son," the fur thing said. "I even remembered the fish."

"Is that really you, Noah?" asked Grandpa.

"Yes, it's me, Noah! Oh... and yes, I am covered in fur."

"How is it possible you grew fur in just a couple hours?" asked Dad, scratching his head.

"To be honest, Dad, I snuck away to the Sasquatch learning center when you, Hunter, and Grandpa and I left to gather food after Mom got upset when I asked about changing my DNA to grow fur like the Sasquatch. In my time frame with the Sasquatches, I have been gone for a year. By your time frame, I have been gone only a few hours. In hindsight, well, I am not sure that I thought this completely through. I was mad, reacted rashly, and will live with my decision for at least another year. I learned how to alter my DNA so I could grow hair like the Sasquatch, and reversing that will take a year. I will be covered with fur for most of a year until my DNA fully reverses the change and my fur falls out."

"I am so mad I could beat you, Noah! But then again, I don't beat animals, so you're safe," Mom said, then fell to the nest floor laughing uncontrollably, and repeating over and over, "He is going to look like a teddy bear for a year! Oh my God, my son is a bear!"

Dad, Hunter, Grandpa, and the freshly fur-covered Noah stared wide-eyed at Mom rolling around in laughter.

"I'm really not sure if she is incredibly upset, or has gone crazy, or is just extremely amused by Noah's poor decision," said Dad "Whatever it is, I plan to maintain a very low profile until I know for sure."

"Noah, I have sure done some bonehead things in my life, but I believe you may have me beat with that doozy of a decision," said Hunter.

"Hey, Noah, can the Sasquatch DNA hair growth technology

work on just the head? Because, I mean, your dad may want to take a break and go to the learning center himself if so." Grandpa asked, then he too started laughing.

Noah started to laugh, and Dad told him if he continued laughing, he was going to take him to a dog groomer and he would get a poodle style cut. Mom had almost regained her composure when she heard Dad threaten Noah with a poodle haircut, then she lost it even more. She was holding her belly and laughing so hard she was crying. "People will be so impressed when I walk Noah around the city on a leash," Mom managed to squeak out in between laughing and crying fits.

"Glad you all think this is so funny. Do any of you have an idea how itchy fur is when it is hot out, or how bad it smells when it gets wet? No wonder the Sasquatch don't swim," Noah whined.

"Oh my God, now I have to take my son to the dog spa," Mom said, and buried her face into his furry chest, "Oh my, you do need a bath, young puppy boy. Grab some soap and hit the shower over there, and don't you be stingy with the soap young pup," mom giggled, and then once more fell into an uncontrollable fit of laughter.

"I'm so very glad everyone is having such a wonderful time at my expense," said Noah.

"Listen, I may not have any experience with the Sasquatch time technology like Noah or Grandpa, but couldn't Noah just go back to the Sasquatch lab and reverse his DNA back to normal? Then he could stay there for the year, or until his hair falls out. When he returns, he can make it so that only a few hours have passed, like you did when you changed your DNA the first time?" asked Hunter.

"No, that's not fair," said Mom, sitting up suddenly and with a serious expression on her face, "I was looking forward to walking Noah around town and taking him to the dog groomer, pet store, and off-leash park!" She did her best to keep a straight face for a few seconds, but then fell backwards into yet another uncontrollable laughing fit.

Noah looked down at his mom on the nest floor, then over to his dad, Hunter, and Grandpa, shook his head, and said, "I am heading to the Sasquatch lab for a year, and by the looks of Mom, I will be back before she stops laughing." His furry little body disappeared quickly down the tree.

5

COMPANY PERSONNEL AND DRONES APPEAR

Ten minutes after Noah left, Grandpa was sitting at the edge of the nest when he heard voices. upon locating their source, he was astonished. Dozens of Sasquatch, along with what appeared to be all 100 missing personnel from Dad's company, were headed towards the wall at the base of the tree. Grandpa yelled and told Dad what was happening. Within seconds, Grandpa was leading the family down to the valley floor. Dad was third down the tree, but first to greet the missing personnel.

The first thing Dad noticed was how healthy and happy they all were. Everyone was talking excitedly about going back home after such a great vacation. What astonished him the most was their drone pilot. He'd had only one leg when Dad last saw him, but now he had two. Looking closer at the rest of the personnel, he began to notice how most looked younger and fitter. No one was obese, or even the least bit overweight.

As a matter of fact, not one of the males was bald or had any amount of hair loss. It was amazing. Everyone looked fantastic.

One of Dad's company leads came up to him to inform him Noah was going to meet them out in the dry riverbed, when they delivered the drones. He explained that, while Noah was waiting for the DNA change to take effect and the fur to drop out, he'd learned to pilot the drones and wanted to fly one out when they were delivered.

"Sounds like Noah is having fun," said Dad, "Although I hope his fur is gone, or I expect his mom will laugh her brains out again, and if the fur is gone, I'm sure she will still be disappointed she can't tease him more."

Dad walked with the company lead to get caught up on what they had been doing ever since the Sasquatch took them. The lead explained that the Sasquatch had ambushed all the drones and captured all the company personnel, and all without anyone getting injured. They'd used some sort of electronic gadget to first render everyone unconscious, and had then carried them carefully to their medical facility. Once in the medical facility, everyone was scanned for any diseases, injuries, or damage. The pilot's leg that they grew back was one of the more dramatic medical miracles they performed. Most of them that were older, out of shape, or had underlying medical issues, had benefited from rejuvenation treatments that reversed aging and cured their many ills. Dad couldn't argue with the results of their medical capabilities. Grandpa was the first patient of the Sasquatch Dad had seen, and now another 100 people had been helped. After the lead finished talking about the medical treatments, Dad asked what kind of training they were getting.

"The Sasquatch training is fantastic! They taught us to live in an environmentally neutral manner, so we won't pollute or need outside energy... each house, and every building, town, or big city can be hooked to a free and clean energy system and from it get unlimited energy. That means no more pollution from greedy power companies or stinking factories. And then, once everyone starts growing the ever-bearing fruits and vegetables the Sasquatch have engineered, no one will ever go hungry again."

The lead then went on to tell of how even though they had been with the Sasquatch for two years, by the time they got back home only hours would have passed, because the Sasquatch didn't want to cause family or company troubles by having them be gone for years in outside time. The personnel would have learned all they needed, but their families and the outside world will not have a clue what has transpired in these woods, so the Sasquatch can continue to help humans without getting bothered by governments. Just as the lead was finishing telling Dad about the Sasquatch controlling time to stay hidden, one of the company experts that had been taken by the Sasquatch strolled up to Dad. This was a computer specialist he had known for 15 years, but who now looked 20 years younger. Her gray hair was not gray any longer, and was instead a luscious dark brown like it had been when they'd first met 15 years ago.

She looked at Dad and said, "You look like you've seen a ghost."

"Well, I have. Or, well, not so much a ghost, but a younger version of Angie, my gifted computer research supervisor, whom I had grown older with, and apparently now is younger again," said Dad, with a surprised smile.

"My changed appearance is nothing compared to the improved health we all have received thanks to living with the Sasquatch," Angie said. "They cured my asthma, and I can jog again. Coming here actually turned out better than collecting a live Sasquatch, since we gained the Sasquatch as friends and teachers. The Sasquatch and I have been in communication with the company. The company is going to diversify into the environmental science field, with our new silent partners being the Sasquatch. They have offered to give us new technology for free that will help clean up the Earth. The company will be buying the property around this valley to protect the Sasquatch from being found out until they are ready to come out to the world. For now, our company will be the sole outlet for their technology. It will all be safe and clean power technology, as well food production. Their goal is to make sure every person on Earth has food, medicine, education, and unlimited clean power to meet their needs."

"Wait a minute," said Dad, "Do you mean to tell me our stuffy company executives have decided to get into the hippy solar and food market? And build in the mountains? So... where are the people going to live, or are they going to commute?" Dad asked, sarcastically.

"Yes, our company executives are going hippy, but only because the money was too tempting to pass up! If someone offered you a million dollars to exercise every day, you would too. It's a reward for doing a healthy thing," said Angie.

"Good point. I guess offering big money to make healthy choices is like paying for good grades, or granting an allowance for doing chores," said Dad.

"My thoughts exactly," said Angie, "In fact, the Sasquatch were so impressed with Hunter and Noah's tree nest design that they asked our company executives if our employees would agree to live in a modified version of Hunter and Noah's design. The new tree designs will have their own power generation systems and be totally weatherproof, but also be capable of having an open nest design on the top. All tree homes will have full recycling, water, and waste disposal systems, similar to a sealed system in a spaceship. Every Sasquatch technology loaded tree home will be as comfortable as a regular human home.

"Oh, please tell me Noah doesn't know about this," Dad pleaded.

"Know about it?! He was the main designer for the Sasquatch. They felt, because of his experience living in the tree, he had the best and most practical ideas about what they needed most. Noah and Hunter showed the Sasquatch that humans can indeed live in environmentally friendly ways like they do, and so came up with a workable plan for all involved.

"Noah's mom isn't going to be so happy about the company moving and having to live in a tree," said Dad.

"Well, since Noah knew he was going to be in for a tough argument with his mom, he designed the tree homes with features that will make her want to live in one," said Angie,

"The bathrooms will have heated and cooled floors and walls to match the seasons, oh, and the showers are *huge* and there are humongous bathtubs. The kitchens come with every gadget you can imagine, and ones you can't... like the food synthesizers, which are capable of making any dish you want—they're kinda like 3D printers, except for food—and best of all is that every tree home comes with robots that clean, cook, and can carry on a conversation. If you desire, robots can even teach you things like music, or schoolwork!"

"I can see my Noah has indeed put a great deal of thought into this venture, and if I were a betting man, I'd put my money on his mom gleefully coming to the valley and happily living in a custom Sasquatch tree home, especially considering those robots that cook and clean," said Dad.

Dad heard a familiar voice coming from the other side of the valley wall they had just reached. The drones were going to be delivered to the dry riverbed, to exactly the spot where they were taken from. If what Grandpa said was true, then the company drones will have been modified by the Sasquatch to be capable of many amazing things, including flying into space, he was thinking, as a hairless Noah clambered over the wall's edge in front of him.

"Hi, Dad, long time no see! Well, at least for me it has been, since it's been another year of my time to maybe an hour of yours. This time I spent my year wisely, training on flying the customized drones. Not to brag, but I have flown in space many times. Oh, and I am hairless again, so Mom won't be mad at me anymore."

"Not to brag! Really... that is not a brag, son. You are such a lucky kid, Noah. I have dreamed of flying into space my whole life," Dad said, with a wistful gaze.

"Don't worry, Dad, I promise to fly you into space on our way home to pack up and move here."

"I am sure you can fly the drone like a pro, but can you imagine what the people at NASA would do? They would have a fit about a 10-year-old boy having flown a Sasquatch modified drone into outer space when they can't!"

"I told him the same thing. Sure enough, he can fly like a champ, but no one can know how well he can fly, or about the Sasquatch, until they are ready to reveal themselves. Then he will be the envy of every kid and adult on earth," said Grandpa.

While Noah was talking to Dad and Grandpa, Mom caught up and got a look at Noah and was relieved to see he was hairless again.

"There's my little hairless boy! But I must say, it really is too bad you're hairless now, Noah, I was getting used to the thought of hanging out at the pet spa and groomers with you as our special bonding time," she said, with a smirk that slowly cracked into a full smile, and soon she was laughing again.

"I was afraid of this," said Noah. "My mom has gone crazy, and now I will have to go live with relatives, because they are going to take her away in a white coat and lock her up in a rubber room!"

Noah couldn't help but grin as he went over and laughed with his mom as they hugged.

6

MOVING TO THE SASQUATCH VALLEY

After all the company personnel and drones were back at the company and everyone had been debriefed, they returned home. The company executives decided to let the personnel tell their families that the company was moving, and where to, but not about the Sasquatch. Those families would all move to the valley, into the Sasquatch custom built tree homes, and when the time was right they would be permitted to learn about them. This was a decision made to support the Sasquatch and their decision not to reveal themselves to the rest of the world until they felt safe. For the time being, the company and the Sasquatch would be building a community together.

Noah flew the drone that his family rode in back to the company. He also flew them into outer space on the way, so they could enjoy weightlessness. Dad was the most excited of the group. Mom couldn't care less about flying in outer space, because it messed up her hair, and she just really wanted to get back home and clean up. Grandpa had already flown into space, so he wasn't too silly, but Hunter was beyond excited. He couldn't stop spinning and tumbling.

"No doubt about it, I am going to be an astronaut when I get older!" Hunter said proudly, then spun off in zero gravity again.

It took a few hours for the company to debrief Dad, Grandpa, and the rest of the family, before they could go home. They had the company lawyers look at the legal paperwork the Sasquatch drew up for Tina. The lawyers were pleased about how the Sasquatch had done such an incredible job and so quickly approved it. Little redhead western girl Tina from the mid 1800s was now officially a young girl visiting from Ohio that was planning on going to school in Washington state, at a gifted school. Or, at least, that's what her government paperwork said.

So far, it looked like the plan to move to the Sasquatch valley was going to go off without a hitch. The company had no problem buying the land in and around it. Next, the company would need to build a factory near the valley. While the company would be building near the valley, they were also going to need to start and build new companies to handle the Sasquatch technology. Full implementation of the plan, and completion of building the factories and companies, was set to take up to 2 years. During that time, the Sasquatch would be growing special trees to customize into homes for the company.

On the way home, Mom was able to tell Tina she had a couple years in human time to get used to the new world before they moved to the Sasquatch valley. During that time, they plan on traveling so Tina could see how humans lived in different places. Tina was excited to see the real world. She had seen pictures and movies of cities and humans, but this would be her first time exploring outside the valley in person. Grandpa stayed at the company to gather his walker, which was being delivered on another drone, while Hunter, Noah, and the rest went home.

Tina's reaction to their house was not what anyone expected. Mom showed Tina every room, and explained what everything was, especially the appliances. When she saw Mom's bathroom, and all the makeup in it, Tina got really excited. She told Mom she remembered some women wore makeup when she was a kid, and the Sasquatch had pictures and movies she had seen with women wearing makeup, but this was the first time she had seen it with her own eyes. Mom promised to make her up when things settled down. Tina looked into the mirror, saw her red hair and freckles, and wished out loud she looked like Mom.

"If you looked like Mom, Hunter wouldn't think you were as cute," said Noah. "I'm pretty sure he likes your freckles and red hair."

Mom was behind Noah when he made that comment, but he suddenly felt her eyes on him and quickly shut his mouth and walked out of the room. One glance at Hunter and it was apparent he was a bit embarrassed, since his face was almost as red as Tina's hair!

Tina, on the other hand, was smiling at Hunter's reaction. She looked at Mom.

"If possible, tomorrow you and I should look closer at the makeup, and maybe try a few colors to see what they look like on me. Hunter, if you want to watch us try makeup and let me know what you think, I would appreciate it very much," Tina said, with a glint in her eye.

"Ah, sure, I wouldn't mind giving my opinion," said Hunter. "I don't know much about makeup, though."

"I don't know makeup either, but it would be nice to have your opinion, Hunter, because you're used to seeing it and know what looks good," she replied with a smile.

It should have been impossible for Hunter to get redder, but after that comment he got so red he almost glowed. Mom saw what was happening and smiled, knowing these two kids were experiencing their first crush. She would have called it 'puppy love,' but after Noah showed up covered in fur, she decided that wasn't a good phrase anymore, and smiled to herself at Noah's silliness earlier. Noah sure has always been a handful, and after having been educated by the Sasquatch, his silliness was accompanied by brilliance. I guess he isn't much different than Grandpa after all, thought Mom.

Tina got the spare bedroom that was upstairs and down the hall from Mom and Dad's. The boys each had a room on the first floor. Tina had not been in a human house for almost 200 years, and the houses were certainly different this century. When Tina was born, there were no refrigerators, clothes washing machines, microwaves, inside toilets, or even running water in most places. The Sasquatch lived very primitively, so Tina was in heaven with all the comforts.

Tina was fascinated by the most basic of everyday comforts, like the water being heated if she wanted. The Sasquatch used lots of water in pools, rivers, baths, and showers, but they never had hot water. Their fur protects them from the cold, so they never needed it. Tina, on the other hand, hated winter baths with the Sasquatch, because no matter how hard the Sasquatch tried, they could never get water that was comfortable enough to bathe in during the winter in the mountains of Washington state.

While Tina was taking a warm soaking bath, she thought of her last time with humans. It had been back when she and her family traveled through Tenino, two days before she was washed down the river. The family had stayed in a hotel with a warm bath then. According to Grandpa, that was over 170 years ago. Now, here she was, bathing in warm water in the same town of Tenino, more than 170 years later. Mom said she moved here when she was a small kid and never wanted to leave. Tina knew she was going to be happy now that she had a family to call her own.

In the morning, Tina went down to the kitchen. When she arrived, everyone had already come down, and even Grandpa was there.

"Hope I did not keep you all waiting," Tina said cheerily, when she saw everyone.

"Not at all, Tina, I only just walked in myself, and the boys' rolled in only seconds ago, so no, you're not late," Grandpa said warmly.

"You're also new here! And we normally do not have set times for breakfast, except on weekends when we are not too busy and want to have family time," Mom added.

"We are about to have a family meeting to go over the details of the company plans regarding moving to the

Sasquatch valley. So far, we know that all employees who choose to stay where they currently live will have the use of drones to commute, and many can work remotely which means that basically their lives will not change. Those employees that want to move to the valley will be getting one of the tree houses for free, and almost everything they need will be provided by the technology that is built in, which the Sasquatch and Noah designed. Every tree will have a garden, its own water and power supply, a food synthesizer, and a 3D printer. The 3D printer will be able to make everything the home occupant needs. They will be able to make shoes, clothes, tools, and building materials... basically anything and everything a person needs to go to the store and buy. The food synthesizer and 3D printer use recycled waste, uneaten food, and even simple dirt to extract the materials needed to build things or make food. The various human space agencies would love to have this technology for their space programs, I'm sure. Anyway, completion of these Sasquatch tree homes will take about 2 years, and in that time we all need to decide if this is what we want to do as a family."

"My request is that we stay together, as a family, and that includes Tina," said Mom.

"At this point, we must all think about our options, keep discussing the merits of each option, and then make our final decisions in the months to come as we learn more," Grandpa said.

"I know for certain that I want to return to go back there and live," said Noah. "I have spent a good deal of time with them and would like to do more studying in their learning centers.

For everyone's information, I don't plan on growing fur again... although I have considered growing myself to 8 feet tall!" Noah was smiling about this and looking like he was serious, but one sideways look from Mom made him rethink it, "But I decided against something that childish," he added, then turned to leave the kitchen.

Before Noah could leave the kitchen, Mom looked at him and realized he hadn't taken his Carhartt coveralls off since they returned the day before, which meant he hadn't removed them since they left. When Mom told him it was time to change clothes, Noah informed her that the Sasquatch had modified his Carhartt's to be self-cleaning. In fact, the suit not only cleaned itself, but also cleaned its wearer as well, so there was no need for Noah to ever change, he told her.

"Noah, I'm pretty sure the Sasquatch did not mean for you to never take your Carhartt coveralls off, and if you don't take them off right now and go take a bath, we will find out if the self-cleaning Carhartt's can remove blood! Your blood!"

Noah ran away from her so fast to bathe that it looked like time slowed for everyone except him! Hunter started laughing, and Mom suggested he may not have his Carhartt's on at that moment, but he certainly could use a bath. Hunter wisely left without a word to go bathe.

"I took a bath last night and this morning, so I am already clean," Tina said to Mom, then started giggling. "I forgot how much fun being with a family can be."

"Well, let's hope your new brothers don't drive you as crazy as they do me," said Mom, with a loving smile.

"It will certainly be a fun two years getting to know the

whole family, and learning about the new human world... I didn't realize how much I missed humans," Tina said quietly, as tears started to form in her eyes.

Mom stepped over to Tina and held her while she cried.

"Don't worry, little one, you have come home now. We have two years to learn, experience, and grow together before we move, so let's make the most of it. That means beginning with breakfast!"

Hunter and Noah returned 15 minutes later, clean enough for Mom's approval, and everyone ate breakfast while planning their futures. They needed to decide if they were going to move, or even if Dad wanted to continue working for the company. Mom had a job to consider, though Grandpa was retired so was free to do anything he chose to. Hunter, Noah, and now Tina needed to consider not just the great Sasquatch learning center, but also the amount of social interaction they needed and wanted.

Dad said, "I have been offered the CEO position of a new division the company is starting near the valley, which specializes in paint. This new paint acts like a solar panel and makes electricity, so anything painted with it can be charged or run by solar power. When a Sasquatch organic battery—which is actually more like a living plant that stores energy like a batter—is added to any toy, house, large building, or even a car, it can power it and only requires a bit of water for the plant, and light for the paint to do so. It is honestly revolutionary, this new Sasquatch technology, and will mean no more pollution from gas motors, coal power plants, and it will even mean power lines won't be needed," Dad said, with pride in his voice.

"Looks like Dad has decided to go back to the valley, and I am also with him," said Noah. "I can see my future will be intertwined with the Sasquatch, and so far, my experience has been unbelievable! So, if it is okay with Mom and Dad, I want to live near the valley, in our tree."

"I'm certain you all know my answer," said Grandpa. "I can't think of a better way to spend my life than learning new science and technology, amongst such wonderful beings as the Sasquatch!"

"A few weeks ago, I would never have even considered living in the woods, in a tree, near 8-foot-tall hairy things. But now, after meeting my new tall hairy friends that only want to help humanity and Tina the wonderful little girl that has joined my family, as well as having learned how incredible it will be living near the valley, I would choose no other place to call home with my family," Mom said, with a little tear of pride in her eye.

"Count me in for moving to our tree," said Hunter. "Once we get there it will be my turn to hit the Sasquatch learning center. After flying in the drone with Noah, I decided I want to train to be a pilot. Maybe once the Sasquatch reveal themselves, I can become a pilot instructor for NASA."

"Although I have spent many years with the Sasquatch, I also want to return to the valley when you all go," said Tina. "The Sasquatch was my family, and after two years studying humans, I'm positive I will want to head back to the valley."

"Looks like we have a unanimous yes vote on moving when the Sasquatch are ready for us," said grandpa. "Since Noah won't be going back to public school, I would like to use his drone piloting skills to ferry me back and forth to the

Sasquatch valley twice a week for my planning meetings," Grandpa added.

"Well, Dad and I are still undecided on what to do with our 10-year-old boy who has multiple PhDs, flies drones into outer space, and has lived with Sasquatch," said Mom. "Although we are quite sure that sending him to 5th grade is not in his, the school's, or the other students' best interest at this time... and probably never will be," Mom added, rolling her eyes.

"For now, we need to take it one day at a time," said Grandpa. "We have two years to prepare, do extra training with the Sasquatch whenever possible, and keep quiet about the Sasquatch until such time that they are ready to reveal themselves."

"Mom, do you think you would reconsider me growing fur again, but with less on my hands, feet, and face?" Noah asked.

Mom turned her head so fast that Noah was sure it would spin off! The look on her face said he'd better make himself scarce. It was going to be a long two years, he thought, as he sprinted out of the kitchen barely ahead of his mom.

ABOUT THE AUTHOR

Patrick Talmadge Sr. has always been a late bloomer. His growth didn't cease until he was over 21 years old. He reached his pinnacle as a national and world-class masters middle-distance runner at the age of 37, when he won his first master's national track and field championship in the 800-meter run.

At 47, Patrick earned his Bachelor of Arts degree and made history as the oldest NCAA cross-country runner. Seven years later, at 54, he returned to college to pursue a Master's degree in Psychology. During this time, he ran the mile in track, once again setting a record as the oldest NCAA track and field runner. He received his Master's degree in Psychology at 57. At the age of 66, he embarked on his writing journey.

Patrick taught himself to read at the tender age of three and a half and has been an avid reader ever since. With a keen interest in all fields of science, science fiction, and fantasy, he amassed a wealth of knowledge that would later prove invaluable when he began writing. Throughout his 20s and 30s, Patrick devoured two to three books a day. Upon graduating from graduate school in 2011, he retired from competitive running and felt a growing desire to write the stories that had been simmering within him.

In November 2021, spurred on by the love of his life, Patrick began his writing career. By July 2023, he had completed an adult four-book science fiction series about Sasquatch, a four-book children's series on the same subject, and a standalone novel about a senior community that befriends a troupe of Sasquatch.

Patrick possesses a unique ability to write multiple stories simultaneously, allowing him to modify and adjust interconnected narratives for clarity when writing a series. With a bit of luck, Patrick will continue to pursue his passion for writing for the rest of his life, or at least until his computer gives out.

ALSO BY PATRICK TALMADGE

Hidden Mountain Chronicles

Sasquatch Race

Sasquatch Prison Diary

Tenino Caverns

Sasquatch Home Planet

Sasquatch Chronicles

Hunter and Noah vs. Sasquatch Vol. 1

Hunter and Noah vs. Sasquatch Vol. 2

Hunter and Noah vs. Sasquatch Vol. 3

Hunter and Noah vs. Sasquatch Vol. 4

Sasquatch Senior Community Series

Sasquatch Senior Community

Sasquatch Senior Community: Lois and Mel the Beginning

Sasquatch Senior Community: The Early Years

Sasquatch Senior Community: The Middle Years

AFTERWORD

Go to hangaripublishing.com to learn more about the Authors and stay up to date with their newest releases.

www.ingramcontent.com/pod-product-compliance
Lightning Source LLC
Chambersburg PA
CBHW061325120626
46546CB00007B/2679